KARATE TEN NO KATA

空手天之 形

HEAVEN SEQUENCE

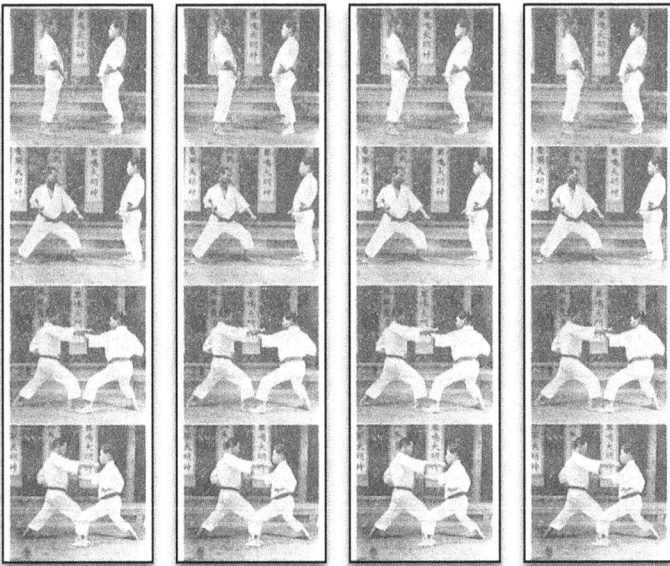

FUNAKOSHI GICHIN

PUBLISHED 1941

TRANSLATED BY ERIC SHAHAN

Translator's Introduction

This is a two sided poster, with each sequence in a vertical column, starting on the right side. The front side is called *Omote*, meaning front, obverse or outer, and the other side is *Ura*, meaning back, reverse or inner.

All information in (brackets) is by the author.

Omote Outer
This side shows solo training

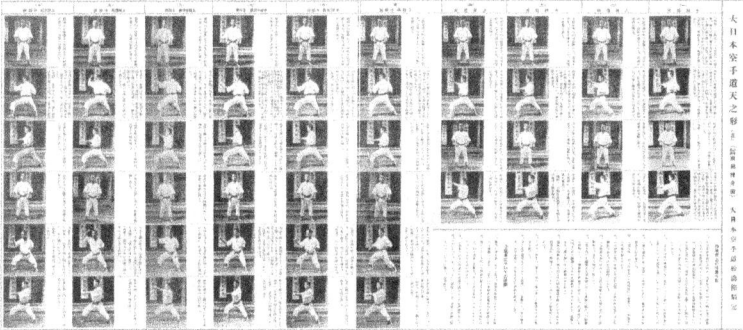

Ura Inner
This side shows how to practice the sequence with a partner

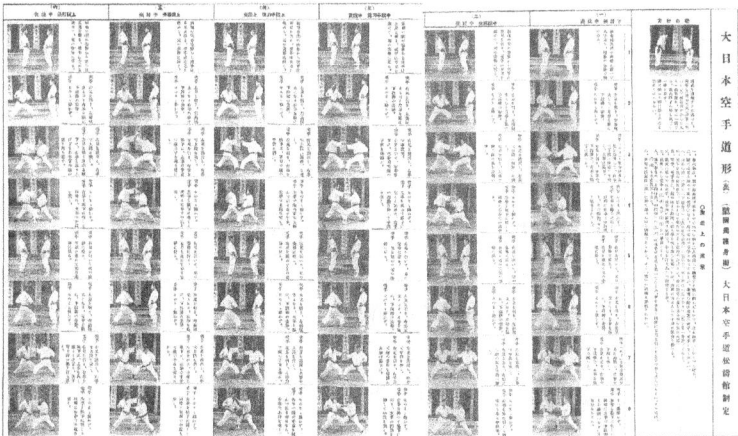

大日本空手道
天之形

東京市豊島区雑司ケ谷六丁目八-一五番地

大日本空手道松濤館

Great Japan Karatedo
Ten no Kata
Heaven Sequence

All Japan Karatedo
Shotokan
Toyoshima-ku, Tokyo City

大日本空手道天之形（表）

（心身鍛錬）國民護身術

大日本空手道松濤館制定

3

Dai Nihon Karatedo Ten no Kata
All Japan Karatedo Heaven Sequence

Omote
Outer

Shinshin Tanren
Forging the Mind and Body

Kokumin Goshin Jutsu
People's Self-Defense

Dai Nihon Karatedo Shotokan
All Japan Karatedo Shotokan

◎演武上の注意十則

一、 大日本空手道天之形は、空手道の形の中から初心者に適當なものを團體演武用として抜萃して編制したものであるが、勿論個人の身心鍛錬用としても十分適切有効なものである事を疑はない。場所も時間も道具も要しない點から昔つても、多事な近代人の運動として是非とも普及せしめたいと思ふ。

二、 この天之形の構成は「突の基本」（一—四）「中段受●突」（五—七）「上段受●突」（八—十）の三部から成つてゐる。

三、 「突の基本」は「逆突」「追突」に分け、其の各を更に中段及上段に分ける。

四、 「立ち方」は「八字立」「後屈立」「前屈立」「不動立」の四種を探つてある。

五、 「中段受●突」は敵が中段を攻撃して來た時の受け方と攻撃法である。之を三種探つてある。

Rules for Training With a Partner

1. The All Japan Karatedo Ten no Kata, Heaven Sequence, was developed from Karatedo techniques that were specifically selected for group practice and adjusted for beginners. Rest assured that this method is effective for solo training to develop the spirit and forge a strong body.

Considering that this method requires no equipment, no space and very little time, it is ideally suited to the busy lives of modern people. I would very much like this method to be adopted widely.

2. The Heaven Sequence is comprised of the following three sections:

Tsuki no Kihon: Basic Strikes (1-4)
Chudan Uke & Tsuki: Middle Blocks and Strikes (5-7)
Jodan Uke Tsuki: Upper Blocks and Strikes (8-10)

3. *Tsuki no Kihon*, Basic Strikes, is divided into:
Gyaku Tsuki: Reverse Punch
Oizuki: Straight Punch
These strikes are further divided into Middle Strikes and Upper Strikes.

4. The four *Tachi Kata*, Ways of Standing, are:
Hachiji Dachi: With the feet spread like the Kanji for eight 八
Kokutsu Dachi: Back Leg Stance, weight is mostly on the back foot.
Zenkutsu Dachi: Front Leg Stance, weight is mostly on the front foot.
Fudo Dachi: Immovable Stance, weight is distributed evenly between both legs.

5. *Chudan Uke Tsuki*, Middle Block and Strike
This is how to block or strike when the opponent attacks your center. Three methods were selected.

六、「上段受・突」は同じく上段を攻撃された時の受け方と攻撃法で、之も三種だけ採つた。

七、「受・突」を練習する時は圖に示した番號の様に、二舉動に分解して、一舉動毎に習熟するがよいが、元來「受け」と「突き」は一舉動となるのを原則するのであるから、熟練したら「受・突」は一舉動にするがよい。

八、演武の回數は十種の形を各二回宛繰返す事になつてゐるが各型左右一回宛とし（一）から（十）まで二回演武してもよい。

九、すべて「突き」「貫き」等の「極め手」の瞬間は十分に氣合を掛ける。

十、常に敵が眼前に在るものと假想して、油斷なく、眼は敵を見つめる心持で、全力をあげて眞剣に演武する事。

6. *Jodan Uke Tsuki*, Upper Block and Strike.
These are the same as the previous Middle Blocks and Strikes except they are how to block and strike when the opponent attacks Jodan, or Upper. Three versions of this were also selected.

7. *Uke Tsuki*, Blocks and Attack. The illustrations are numbered sequentially and show these as two different moves, and each should be trained extensively. However, as the Block and Strike are fundamentally one movement, once you have practiced them thoroughly the two movements should be done as one action.

8. As far as repetition goes, this training method has ten steps and each is done twice, once for each arm. I recommend starting from 1 and proceeding to 10, which will train each arm, and doing the whole sequence twice.

9. For each *Kiwame-te*, Ultimate Move, whether it is a Strike or Thrust, be sure to use a Kiai, shout unifying the body and intent, at the moment of impact.

10. You should always envision the opponent is right before your eyes. Your eyes should be forward as if focused on that enemy, without faltering. Train seriously, with all the power you can muster.

○寫眞についての注意

一、動作を分り易く見せる爲に、用意の姿勢だけはすべて正面から撮影し「突き」「受け」の姿勢は左側面から撮影した

二、隨つて(1)から(2)への動作の續き方が分りにくいかも知れぬが、(1)の用意の姿勢を、向つて左方を向いてゐるものとして(2)へつづけて見て頂きたい。

三、「突き」から「用意」の姿勢に戻るところも同様である。

四、(一)を「1、2、3、4」と演武したら、用意の姿勢(即ち(二)の1〕に移る。以下同じ。

Things to Remember When Viewing the Photographs

1. To make the movements easier to understand the *Yoh-i*, Ready Stance, will always be shown from the front. The strikes and blocks have been photographed from the left side.

2. Thus the way the movements transition from (1) to (2) can be somewhat confusing, however please understand that after (1) which shows the Yoh-i, Ready Stance, the following picture (2) will be from the side and show the next step.

3. The transition from the final strike back to Ready Stance will be done in the same way.

4. Part One of this sequence has four steps. After training steps 1,2,3 & 4 you will return to Ready Stance, which is also step 1 of Part Two of the sequence. The rest of the sequence will continue in the same manner.

（一）

中段追突

「用意」の號令で「八字立」の姿勢、即ち左圖の樣に左右の拳を握つて腿の前に構へ、左足、右足の順に爪先を八字形に開いて立つ。（注意）兩肩を下げ、視線は眼の高さ。

右足を一歩前に踏出して圖の樣に「右前屈立」となり、左拳を脇下に引きつけると同時に、右拳を前方かへる。〈胸の高さに突き出す。〉（注意）突き出す拳は、一度腰に引いてから突出す。

右足を元の位置に引くと同時に、左右の拳を下して、用意の姿勢に（注意）この動作はユックリ重々しく。

左足を一歩前に踏出し「左前屈立」となり乍ら右拳を脇下に引きつけ左拳を前方鳩尾の位置に突出す。（注意）前屈の時は左右の爪先を同方向に向ける。前の足は膝から下垂直に。後の足は膝を伸ばす。

1. *Chudan Oizuki* Middle Strike	
	At the command of 「*Yoh-i!* Ready!」 go into 「Hachiji no Kurai, Standing with your feet like the Kanji for Eight 八」 This is shown in the picture. Your left and right hands are squeezed into fists in front of your thighs. Starting with the toes of your left foot, followed by the toes of your right foot, position your feet in Hachi Ji Gata, or Shaped Like the Kanji Eight. (Caution) Allow your shoulders to droop, you should be looking directly into the eyes of your opponent.
	Step forward with your right foot and take 「Migi Zenkutsu Dachi, Right Front Stance」 as shown in the picture. Pull your left fist back below your armpit and, at the same time, punch forward with your right fist at chest-level. (Caution) The fist you are punching with should be pulled back to your waist before striking.
	Pull your right foot back to the starting position and, at the same time, lower your fists, returning to Yoh-i no Shisei, Ready Stance. (Caution) This movement should be slow and dignified.
	Step forward with your left foot and go into 「Hidari Zenkutsu Dachi, Left Front Stance」 as you pull your right fist under your armpit and punch forward with your left fist to the opponent's solar plexus. (Caution) When going into Zenkutsu stance, the toes of both feet should be pointing the same direction. The toes of the front foot should be directly under the knee. The back knee should be extended straight.

（二）

上 段 追 突

中段追突の(4)の姿勢から、左足を右足を一歩踏出し、右前屈立とな引き、左右の拳を下ろし、用意のり、左を脇下に引きつけると同時姿勢に戻る。に、右拳を顔面の高さに突き出す。

右足を引き、左右の拳を下ろして用意の姿勢に戻る。

左足を一歩踏出し、左前屈立となり、右拳を脇下に、左拳を顔面の高さに突き出す。

2. *Jodan Oizuki* Upper Strike

After punching with Chudan Oizuki, Middle Straight Punch (picture 4) pull your left foot back and drop both fists down, retuning to Yoh-i, Ready stance.

Step forward with your right foot, taking Migi Zenkutsu Dachi, Right Front Stance. Pull your left back under your armpit and, at the same time, punch with your right fist at the height of Ganmen, the Face.

Pull your right foot back and lower your fists, returning to Yoh-i, Ready stance.

Step forward with your left foot, taking Hidari Zenkutsu Dachi, Left Front Stance. Pull your right fist back under your armpit and, at the same time, punch with your left fist at the height of Ganmen, the Face.

（三）中段逆突

上段追突の(4)の姿勢から、左足を引き、左右の拳を下ろして、用意の姿勢に戻る。

右足を一歩前に踏出して不動立になると同時に左拳を脇下に、右拳を中段に突出す。

（注意）左足を出し、右拳で突くので逆突といふ、拳は腰を捻る氣持で突出す。

左足を元の位置に引き、左右の拳を下ろして用意の姿勢に戻る。

右足を一歩踏出して不動立になると同時に、右拳脇下に、左拳を中段に突出す。

（注意）不動立は両足とも膝を十分曲げて腰を落す。

3. *Chudan Gaykuzuki Oizuki* Middle Reverse Strike

After punching with Jodan Oizuki, Upper Strike (picture 4) pull your left foot back and drop both fists down. You have now returned to Yoh-i, Ready stance.

Step forward with your left foot and go into Fudo Dachi, Immovable Stance. At the same time pull your left fist under your armpit and strike with Chudan, Middle Strike, with your right fist.
(Caution) Stepping forward with your left and striking with your right is called a Gyaku Tsuki, Reverse Strike. You should twist your hips as you punch.

Pull your left foot back and lower your fists, returning to Yoh-i, Ready Stance.

Step forward with your right foot and go into Fudo Dachi, Immovable Stance. At the same time pull your right fist under your armpit and strike with Chudan, Middle Strike, with your left fist.
(Caution) Correct Fudo Dachi means lowering your hips and bending your knees sufficiently.

（四）
上段逆突

中段逆突の(4)の姿勢から、右足を引き、左右の拳を下ろして、用意の姿勢に戻る。

左足を踏出して不動立になると同時に、左拳を脇下に、右拳を上段に突き出す。

左足を元の位置に引き、左右の拳を下ろして用意の姿勢に戻る。

右足を一歩踏出して不動立になると同時に、右拳を脇下に、左拳を上段に突出す。

4. *Jodan Gaykuzuki Oizuki* Upper Reverse Strike

	After punching with Chudan Gaykuzuki Oizuki, Middle Reverse Strike (picture 4) pull your right foot back and drop both fists down, retuning to Yoh-i, Ready stance.
	Step forward with your left foot and go into Fudo Dachi, Immovable Stance. At the same time pull your left fist under your armpit and strike with Jodan, Upper Strike, with your right fist.
	Pull your left foot back and lower your fists, returning to Yoh-i, Ready Stance.
	Step forward with your right foot and go into Fudo Dachi, Immovable Stance. At the same time pull your right fist under your armpit and strike with Jodan, Upper Strike, with your left fist.

（五）
下段拂中段突

上段逆突の(4)の姿勢から右足を引き、左右の拳を下ろして、用意の姿勢に戻る。

右足を一歩後に引き不動立となり（以下すべて同じ右拳を脇下に引きつけ、左拳を右肩前から斜め下に打ち下ろす。
（注意）敵が下段（下腹）を突いて來たと假想して左手首で打拂ふ。

右脇の拳を中段に突き出すと同時に、左拳を脇下に引きつける。
（注意）この姿勢は即ち中段逆突である。

右足を元の位置に進め、左右の拳を下ろして用意の姿勢に戻る。

左足を一歩後へ引き、左拳を脇下に引きつけ、右拳は左肩前から斜め下に打ち拂ふ。

（注意）右拳は右膝頭の上七八寸の所で打ち止める。

左拳を中段に突出すと同時に、右拳を脇に引拳。

（注意）不動立となり、腰を捻つて突出す事。

5 *Gedan Harai Chudan Tsuki*
Lower Sweep, Middle Strike (1-3)

After punching with Jodan Gaykuzuki Oizuki, Upper Reverse Strike (picture 4) pull your right foot back and drop both fists down, retuning to Yoh-i, Ready stance.

Pull your right foot back one step and go into Fudo Dachi, Immovable Stance. (From here on it will be the same.) Pull your right fist back so it is under your armpit and swing your left fist down diagonally from your right shoulder. This action is called Uchi Oroshi, Dropping Strike.
(Caution) In this situation we are imagining your opponent is striking to Gedan (the lower abdomen) and you are responding by blocking and sweeping this strike away with your left wrist.

Strike to Chudan with your right fist, which you have been holding below your right armpit. At the same time pull your left fist back below your left armpit.
(Caution) The position you have now taken is, in other words, Chudan Gyaku Tsuki, Reverse Middle Strike.

Gedan Harai Chudan Tsuki
Lower Sweep, Middle Strike (4-6)

Step forward with your right foot so you return to your original position. Lower your fists, returning to Yoh-i, Ready stance.

Pull your left foot back one step and move your right fist back so it is under your armpit. Swing your right fist down diagonally from your left shoulder in an Uchi Harau, Striking Sweep.
(Caution) Your right fist should strike and stop 7 or 8 Sun, 21~24 centimeters above your right knee.

Strike to Chudan with your left fist and, at the same time, pull your right fist back below your right armpit.
(Caution) You are now in Fudo Dachi, Immovable Stance. Twist your hips as you launch your strike.

（六）
中段受腕　中段突

前項(6)の姿勢から、左足を元の位置に進め、左右の拳を下ろして用意の姿勢に戻る。

右足を後へ引いて不動立となり、右拳を脇に引くと同時に、左肘を半ば曲げて右肩前から左肩前方に向つて打ち拂ふ。

（注意）　手の甲は外を向く。

左拳を脇に引きつけると同時に、右拳で中段を突く。

右足を元の位置に進め、左右の拳を下ろして用意の姿勢に戻る。

左足を一歩後へ引き左拳を脇にとり、右肘を半ば曲げて左肩前から右肩の前方へ向つて打ち拂ふ。

（注意）この時右拳は肩の高さ。

右拳を脇に引きつけると同時に、左拳で中段を突く。

6. *Chudan Ude Uke, Chudan Tsuki*
Mid-level Arm Block, Middle Strike (1-3)

This starts from the previous position (picture 6.) Step forward with your left foot to your original starting point. Lower your fists, returning to *Yoh-i*, Ready stance.

Pull your right foot back and take Fudo Dachi, Immovable stance. Pull your right fist back so it is under your armpit and, at the same time, bend your left elbow halfway. Swing your arm in a sweeping motion starting from in front of your right shoulder to strike in front of your left shoulder.
(Caution) The back of your hand should be facing outward.

Pull your left fist back so it is below your armpit and, at the same time, punch Chudan with your right fist.

Chudan Ude Uke Chudan Tsuki
Mid-level Arm Block, Middle Strike (4-6)

Step forward with your right foot so you return to your original position. Lower your fists, returning to *Yoh-i*, Ready stance.

Step back with your left foot and pull your left fist back so it is under your armpit. Bend your right elbow halfway. Swing your arm in a sweeping motion from in front of your left shoulder to strike in front of your right shoulder.
(Caution) Your right fist should be at shoulder height.

Pull your right fist back so it is under your armpit and, at the same time, punch Chudan, the center of your opponent, with your left fist.

（七）

貫段中　受刀手段中

前項(6)の姿勢から左足を元の位置に進めて、用意の姿勢に戻る。

右足を後へ引いて後屈立となり、右拳を脇に引きつけると同時に、左手を手刀として、右肩前方から肘を半ば曲げたまゝ左肩前方に向つて打ち排ふ。

（注意）後屈立は不動立に似てゐるが軆の重心を後の足で支へる心持、膝は十分に曲げる事。

左手を握つて脇に引きつけると同時に、右手を開き、貫手として中段を突く。

（注意）手刀と貫手は同じ形だが使用する部分が邁ふのである。

右足を元の位置に進め、用意の姿勢に戻る。

左足を引いて後屈立となり、左拳を脇に引きつけ右手を手刀として肘を半ば曲げたまゝ左肩前から右肩前に向つて打ち拂ふ。

（注意）手刀の指先は肩の高さ、中段突を受ける心持。

右手を握って、脇に引きつけると同時に、左貫手で敵の中段を突く。

（注意　貫手とは指頭で貫くといふ意味である。

7. *Chudan Shuto Uke, Chudan Nuki*
Mid-level Knife Hand Block, Middle Piercing Strike (1-3)

This starts from the previous position (picture 6.) Step forward with your left foot to your original starting point. Lower your fists, returning to *Yoh-i*, Ready stance.

Step back with your right foot so you are standing in Kokutsu Dachi, Back Stance, and pull your right fist back so that it is under your armpit. At the same time, with your left hand, strike with a Shuto, Knife Hand. Starting from in front of your right shoulder, do a sweeping strike that stops in front of your left shoulder. Your elbow should be bent as you do this strike.

(Caution) While Kokutsu Dachi, Back Stance, may look like Fudo Dachi, Immovable Stance, in this case your body weight is on your back foot and your knees are bent sufficiently.

Close your left hand into a fist and pull it back below your armpit. Open your right hand and strike Chudan, Middle, with Nuki-te, Piercing Strike.

(Caution) While the shape of Shuto and Nuki-te are the same, the point you are striking is different.

Chudan Ude Uke Chudan Tsuki
Mid-level Arm Block, Middle Strike (4-6)

Step forward with your right foot so you return to your original position. Lower your fists, returning to *Yoh-i*, Ready stance.

Step back with your left foot so you are standing in Kokutsu Dachi, Back Stance, and pull your left fist back so that it is below your armpit. At the same time, with your right hand, strike with a Shuto. This strike starts in front of your left shoulder and sweeps out, stopping in front of your right shoulder. Be sure to keep your elbow bent.
(Caution) When striking with Shuto, the ends of your fingers should be at shoulder level.

Close your left hand in a fist and pull it back below your armpit. At the same time, open your left hand and strike your opponent Chudan, Middle, with Nuki-te, Piercing Strike.
(Caution) The meaning of Nuki-te is to penetrate through with the ends of the fingers.

（八）
突段上　拂刀手段上

前項(6)の姿勢から左足を元の位置に進めて、用意の姿勢に戻る。

右足一歩後へ引き、右拳を脇に引きつけ、左手を手刀として、肘を半ば曲げ、眼の高さに打ち拂ふ。

（注意）上段突きを打ち拂ふ心持ち。

左手を握つて脇下に引きつけると同時に右拳で上段を突く。

右足を進めて元の位置にかへし、用意の姿勢に戻る。

左足を引き、左拳を脇に引きつけると同時に、右手刀で上段を拂ふ

右手を握って脇に引きつけると同時に左拳で上段を突く。

8. *Jodan Shuto Harai, Jodan Tsuki*
Upper-Level Knife Hand Sweep, Upper Level Strike (1-3)

This starts from the previous position (picture 6.) Step forward with your left foot to your original starting point. Lower your fists, returning to *Yoh-i*, Ready stance.

Step back with your right foot, and pull your right fist back so that it is under your armpit. At the same time, with your left hand, strike with a Shuto. Keeping your elbow bent and starting from in front of your right shoulder, do a sweeping strike at eye level.

(Caution) This should be done with the feeling of striking and sweeping away a Jodan Tsuki, Upper Strike.

Squeeze your left hand into a fist and pull it back under your armpit and, at the same time, strike to Jodan, Upper, with your right fist.

Chudan Ude Uke Chudan Tsuki
Mid-level Arm Block, Middle Strike (4-6)

Step forward with your right foot so you return to your original position. Lower your fists, returning to *Yoh-i*, Ready stance.

Pull your left leg back while pulling your left fist back below your armpit. At the same time, sweep to Jodan, Upper, with your right Shuto.

Squeeze your right hand into a fist and pull it back under your armpit. At the same time, strike to Jodan, Upper, with your left fist.

（九）

上段揚受　中段突

前項(6)の姿勢から左足を元の位置に進めて、用意の姿勢に戻る。

右足を一歩後へ引き、右拳を脇に引きつけると同時に、左拳を半ば肘を曲げ手甲を内側とし、額上に拂ひ揚げる。

（注意）揚げた拳は額から五六寸の所にある。

左拳を脇に引きつけると同時に、右拳で中段を突く。

右足を元の位置に進め、用意の姿勢に戻る。

左足を後へ引き、左拳を脇に引きつけ、右拳を肘を半ば曲げて手甲を内側にし額上に拂ひ揚げる。

（注意）肘が上りすぎぬ様。拳の下から敵を見る心持。

右拳を脇に引きつけると同時に、左拳を中段に突き出す。

9. *Jodan Age Uke, Chudan Tsuki*
Upper Rising Block, Middle Strike (1-3)

This starts from the previous position (picture 6.) Step forward with your left foot to your original starting point. Lower your fists, returning to *Yoh-i*, Ready stance.

Pull your right foot one step back, drawing your right fist below your armpit. At the same time, sweep your left fist up above your forehead. Your elbow should be bent with your Te-no-ko, or the back of your hand, facing inward.
(Caution) Your fist should be about 5 or 6 Sun, 15 ~ 18 centimeters from your forehead.

Pull your left fist back below your armpit and, at the same time punch Chudan, Middle, with your right fist.

Chudan Ude Uke Chudan Tsuki
Mid-level Arm Block, Middle Strike (4-6)

Step forward with your right foot so you return to your original position. Lower your fists, returning to *Yoh-i*, Ready stance.

Pull your left foot back and draw your left fist below your armpit. Sweep your right fist up above your forehead. You should keep your elbow bent and the back of your hand facing inward.
(Caution) Be sure not to raise your elbow too high. You should be able to keep your opponent in sight just below your fist.

Pull your right fist back below your armpit and, at the same time, strike Chudan, Middle, with your left fist.

（十）

上段打込 中段突

前項(6)の姿勢から左足を元の位置に進めて、用意の姿勢に戻る。

右足一歩後へ引き、右拳を脇に引きつけると同時に、左拳を頭上高く振りあげざま、目の前に打ち下ろす。

（注意）手の甲は外側、拳の位置は目の前一尺位、やゝ見下す程度

左拳を脇に引きつけると同時に、右拳で中段を突く。

40

8. *Jodan Shuto Harai, Jodan Tsuki*
Upper-Level Knife Hand Sweep, Upper Level Strike (1-3)

This starts from the previous position (picture 6.)   Step forward with your left foot to your original starting point. Lower your fists, returning to *Yoh-i*, Ready stance.

Pull your right foot back one step and draw your right fist back below your armpit. At the same time, swing your left fist high above your head and strike down, ending at eye level.
(Caution) Your Te-no-ko, or the back of your hand, should be facing away from you. Your fist should be positioned at eye level about 1 Shaku, 30 centimeters, in front of you and angled slightly downward.

Pull your left fist back under your armpit and, at the same time, strike Chudan, Middle, with your right fist.

Chudan Ude Uke Chudan Tsuki
Mid-level Arm Block, Middle Strike (4-6)

Step forward with your right foot so you return to your original position. Lower your fists, returning to *Yoh-i*, Ready stance.

Step forward with your left foot one step and pull your left fist back under your armpit. At the same time swing your right fist up high above your head before striking down in front of you. The strike should end in front of your eyes.
(Caution) When striking down be sure that your strike is descending diagonally from above your head.

Pull your right fist back under your armpit and, at the same time punch to Chudan, Middle, with your left fist.

大日本空手道形（裏）

（心身鍛錬）國民護身術

大日本空手道松濤館制定

Dai Nihon Karatedo Kata
All Japan Karatedo Sequence

Ura
Inner

Shinshin Tanren
Forging the Mind and Body

Kokumin Goshin Jutsu
People's Self-Defense

Dai Nihon Karatedo Shotokan Seitei
Developed by All Japan Karatedo Shotokan

禮 の 仕 方

演武を開始するに當つて、突手を（向つて左）受手（向つて右）兩者向ひ合つて凡そ一間程離れ、互に一禮する。演武終了の時も同じく一禮を交す。禮に始つて禮に終るの心を忘れてはならない。

Rei no Shikata
How to Bow

When beginning practice the Tsuki-te, or Attacker, (on the left) and the Uke-te, or Defender, (on the right) face each other and bow. They should stand about 1 Kan, 180 centimeters, apart and bow. At the end of practice they should also exchange a bow in the same fashion. You should never forget :

Rei ni Hajimette Rei ni Owaru
You should begin with a bow and end with a bow.

○演武上の注意

一、裏六本は、表の第五以下第十までの六つの形を二人相對して練習する様に組んだもので、之を組手（くみて）と呼ぶ。

二、圖では常に向つて左が突手になり、向つて右が受手となつてゐるが、練習の際は交互に突手、受手となるがよい。

三、突手の拂へは常に「下段拂ひ」（表の第五參照）の姿勢で、突く時は「追ひ突を」（表の第一參照）である。

四、受手は表の第五以下、第十までの形をそのまゝ演武すればよい。

五、突手、受手共に、技の極まる瞬間（即ち拳を突き出した時）には、丹田に力を入れて十分に氣合を掛ける。

六、演武に當つては突手、受手共に眞劍な氣持で、全力を打ち込んで動作する事。

七、熟練したら受手は(3)(4)及び(7)(8)を一擧動とする。

八、裏六本目の「上段打込、中段突」の(3)(4)は受手が左足を引いてゐるが、表十本目と同樣に右足を引いて左手で打ち込んでもよい。その時は、(7)(8)も左右反對となる。

九、其他の注意は「表」に於て述べたのと同樣であるから、よく「表」の説明を參照されたい。

Cautions to Remember When Training

1. The Ura Roppon, or Inner Six Techniques, consists of techniques 5 ~ 10 from the Outer side of this sheet. They have been combined into a training method for two practitioners. This is called Kumite, or paired training. The Kanji 組手 are read as (Ku-Mi-Te.)

2. The illustrations will always show the Tsuki-te, Attacker, on the left and the Uke-te, or Defender on the right. However, when training, it is best that partners alternate between Tsuki-te and Uke-te.

3. The Tsuki-te, Attacker, will adopt the stance Gedan Harai, Lower Sweep (see step 5 on the Outer section) When striking he will use Oizuki, Straight Punch. (See step 1 in the Outer section.)

4.The Uke-te, Defender, should practice the techniques shown in steps 5 ~ 10 on the Outer section. Do not forget that you should always maintain eye contact with your training partner.

5. Both the Attacker and Defender should put power in Tanden at the moment of contact. (In other words when you strike with your fist.) In addition, be sure to use powerful Kiai, a shout unifying body and intent.

6. When training, both the Attacker and Defender should maintain the feeling of Shinken, a real fight, and strike with all the power they can generate.

7. A Defender who is Jukuren, or has trained extensively, should combine movements (3) & (4) as well as (7) & (8) into one movement.

8. In steps (3) & (4) of the sixth Inner technique Jodan Uchi Komi, Chudan Tsuki, Upper Strike, Middle Strike you should pull your left leg back, however, as shown in step 10 on the Outer, you can also pull your right foot back and strike with your left fist. If you do so the left and right feet will be reversed when doing steps (7) & (8.)

9. For other cautions, refer to what was written on the Outer side of the page, as all that information applies as well. I encourage everyone to review the material written on the Outer side of this document thoroughly.

（二）

下段拂中段突

兩者約三尺の距離を置いて八字立ち、用意の姿勢で向ひ合ふ。

突手　右足を引き、左前屈立となり右拳を脇に下段拂の姿勢。

受手　そのまゝ動かず。

突手　「エイ」と氣合諸共右足を踏出して、右拳で下段（腹部）を突く。左拳は脇下。

受手　右足を引き、左拳で下段拂ひ、右拳を脇下に構へる。

突手　そのまゝ動かず。

受手　左拳を脇下に引くと同時に右拳で中段突き。その瞬間「ヤッ」と氣合をかける。

突手　右足を引いて、元の
姿勢に戻る。

受手　右足を進めて元の姿
姿に戻る。

突手　左足を引き、右前屈
立となり、左拳を脇
に、下段拂の姿勢。

受手　そのまゝ動かず。

突手「エイ」と氣合諸共左
足を踏出し、左拳で
下段を突く。

受手　左足を引き、右拳で
下段拂ひ、左拳を脇
下に構へる。

突手　その儘動かず、

受手　右拳を脇下に引くと
同時に左拳で中段突
その瞬間「ヤッ」と
氣合をかける。

1. *Gedan Harai, Chudan Tsuki*
Lower Sweep, Middle Strike

1. Both you and your training partner stand in Yoh-i no Shisei, Ready Stance, about 3 Shaku, 90 centimeters, apart from each other. You both stand with your feet in Hachiji Dachi, pointed outwards like the Kanji for eight 八.

2. The Tsuki-te, Attacker, should pull his right leg back, moving his legs into Hidari Zenkutsu Dachi, Left Front Stance. With his right fist tucked below his armpit he positions himself in Gedan Harai, Lower Sweep.
You, the Uke-te or Defender, stay in the same position and do not move.

3. The Attacker shouts a Kiai of *Ei!* as he steps forward with his right foot and strikes to Gedan (the abdomen) with his right fist. His left fist should be under his left armpit.
Respond by pulling your right foot back and do a Gedan Harai, Lower Sweep, with your left hand. Pull your right fist back under your right armpit.

4. The Attacker remains in that position and does not move.
Pull your left fist back under your armpit. At the same time, strike to Chudan, Middle, with your right fist. You should shout a Kiai of *Ya!* the moment you strike.

1. *Gedan Harai, Chudan Tsuki*
Lower Sweep, Middle Strike

5. The Attacker pulls his right foot back, returning to his original position.
You step forward with your right foot, returning to your original position.

6. The Attacker pulls his left leg back, going into Migi Zenkutsu Dachi, Right Front Stance. His left fist is under his armpit and he is standing in Gedan Harai, Lower Sweep.
You remain in that position and do not move.

7. The Attacker shouts a Kiai of *Ei!* and, at the same time, steps forward with his left foot and strikes Gedan, Lower, with his left fist.
You respond by pulling your left foot back and defending with a Gedan Harai, Lower Sweep, with your right fist. Pull your left fist back under your armpit.

8. The Attacker remains in place and does not move.
You pull your right fist back under your armpit and, at the same time, strike to Chudan, Middle, with your left fist. The moment you strike you should shout a Kiai of *Ya!*

（二）

中段腕受　中段突

前項の(8)の姿勢から突手は左足を引き、受手は左足を進めて、元の姿勢に戻る。

突手　右足を引き、左前屈立となり右拳を脇に下段拂の姿勢。

受手　そのまゝ動かず。

突手　右足を踏出し、右拳で中段（鳩尾）を突く。

受手　右足を引き、左拳の腕で敵の腕を外側へ弾く。

突手　そのまゝ動かず。

受手　左拳を脇下に引くと同時に右拳で中段突き。

54

突手　右足を引いて、元の
姿勢に戻る。
受手　右足を進めて元の姿
勢に戻る。

突手　左足を引き、右前屈
立となり、左拳を脇
に、下段拂の姿勢。
受手　そのまゝ動かず。

突手　左足を踏出し、左拳
で中段を突く。
受手　左足を引き、右腕に
て敵の腕を外側へ彈
く。

突手　そのまゝ動かず。
受手　右拳を脇に引くと同
時に左拳で中段突。

2. *Chudan Ude Uke, Chudan Tsuki*
Middle Arm Block, Middle Strike

1. Continuing from step 8 of the previous technique, the Attacker pulls his left foot back while you, the Defender, step forward with your left foot. You both have returned to the starting position.

2. The Attacker pulls his right leg back, moving his legs into Hidari Zenkutsu Dachi, Left Front Stance. With his right fist tucked below his armpit, he positions himself in Gedan Harai, Lower Sweep.
You stay in the same position and do not move.

3. The Attacker steps forward with his right foot and strikes to Chudan, Middle. (Mizo-Ochi, the solar plexus.)
Respond by pulling your right foot back and, with your left hand in a fist, swing your arm and knock the Attacker's arm to the outside.

4. The attacker stays in that position and does not move.
Next, you pull your left hand back under your armpit and, at the same time, strike to Chudan, Middle, with your right fist.

2. *Chudan Ude Uke, Chudan Tsuki*
Middle Arm Block, Middle Strike

5. The Attacker pulls his right leg back, returning to his original position.
You step forward with your right foot, returning to your starting position.

6. The Attacker pulls his left foot back and goes into Migi Zenkutsu Dachi, Right Front Stance, with his left fist under his armpit. He stands in Gedan Harai, Lower Sweep.
You remain as you are, not moving.

7. The Attacker steps forward with his left foot and strikes to Chudan, Middle, with his left fist.
Respond by pulling your left foot back and using your right arm to knock your opponent's arm to the outside.

8. The Attacker stays in that position and doesn't move.
You pull your right fist back under your armpit and, at the same time, strike to Chudan, Middle, with your right fist.

（三）
中段手刀受　中段貫

前項の(8)の姿勢から突手は左足を引き、受手は左足を進めて、元の姿勢に戻る。

突手　右足を引き、左前屈立となり右拳を脇に下段拂の姿勢。

受手　そのまゝ動かず。

突手　右足を踏出し、右拳で中段突。

受手　右足を引き、右拳脇下に、左手刀で敵の手首を切拂ふ。

突手　そのまゝ動かず。

受手　左手を握って脇下に引くと同時に、右手の四指を伸して中段を突く。

突手　右足を引いて、元の
姿勢に戻る。
受手　足を進めて元の姿
勢に戻る。

突手　左足を引き、右前屈
立となり、左拳を脇
に、下段拂の姿勢。
受手　そのまゝ動かず。

突手　左足を踏出し、左拳
で中段を突く。
受手　左足を引き、右手刀
で敵の手首を切拂ふ
左拳は脇下に。

突手　そのまゝ動かず。
受手　右手を握つて脇下に
引き、左手の四指を
伸して中段を突く。

3. *Chudan Shuto Uke, Chudan Nuki*
Middle Knife Hand Block, Middle Piercing Strike

1. Continuing from step 8 of the previous technique, the Attacker pulls his left foot back while you, the Defender, step forward with your left foot. You both have returned to the starting position.

2. The Attacker pulls his right foot back, moving his legs into Hidari Zenkutsu Dachi, Left Front Stance. He pulls his right fist under his armpit and takes Gedan Harai, Lower Sweep, stance.
You remain in the same position and do not move.

3. The Attacker steps forward with his right foot and strikes to Chudan, Middle. Respond by pulling your right foot back and pulling your right fist under your armpit. With your left hand in a Shuto, Knife Hand, strike the Attacker's wrist with a Kiri-Harau, Sweeping Cut.

4. The Attacker remains in this position and does not move.
You squeeze your left hand into a fist and pull it back under your armpit. At the same time, extend the four fingers of your right hand and strike to Chudan, Center.

3. *Chudan Shuto Uke, Chudan Nuki*
Middle Knife Hand Block, Middle Piercing Strike

5. The Attacker pulls his right foot back, returning to his original stance.
You step forward and also return to your original stance.

6. The Attacker pulls his left foot back, moving his legs into Migi Zenkutsu Dachi, Right Front Stance. He pulls his left fist back under his armpit and goes into Gedan Harai.
You remain in the same position and do not move.

7. The Attacker steps forward with his left foot and strikes to Chudan, Middle, with this left fist.
You respond by pulling your left foot back and, with your right hand in a Shuto, Knife Hand, strike the Attacker's wrist with a Kiri-Harau, Sweeping Cut. At the same time, you pull your left fist under your armpit.

8. The Attacker remains in that position and does not move.
Squeeze your right hand into a fist and pull it back under your armpit. Extend the four fingers of your left hand and strike to Chudan, Middle.

（四）
上段手刀拂　上段突

前項の(8)の姿勢から突手は左足を引き、受手は左足を進めて、元の姿勢に戻る。

突手　右足を引き、左前屈立となり右拳を脇に下段拂の姿勢。
受手　そのまゝ動かず。

突手　右足を踏出し、右拳で上段（顔面）を突く。
受手　右足を引き、右拳を脇下に、手刀で敵の手首を拂ふ。

突手　そのまゝ動かず。
受手　左手で敵の手首を掴んで引き寄せ乍ら、右拳で上段を突く。

突手　右足を引いて、元の姿勢に戻る。

受手　右足を進めて元の姿勢に戻る。

突手　左足を引き、右前屈立となり、左拳を腋に、下段挑の姿勢。

受手　そのまゝ動かず。

突手　左足を踏出し左拳で上段を突く。

受手　左足を引き、右手刀で敵の手首を挑ふ。

突手　そのまゝ動かず。

受手　右手で敵の手首を掴んで引き寄せ乍ら、左拳で上段を突く。

4. *Jodan Shuto Harai, Jodan Tsuki*
Upper Knife Hand Sweep, Upper Strike

1. Continuing from step 8 of the previous technique, the Attacker pulls his left foot back while you, the Defender, step forward with your left foot. You both have returned to the starting position.

2. The Attacker pulls his right foot back, moving his legs into Hidari Zenkutsu Dachi, Left Front Stance. With his right fist under his armpit he stands in Gedan Harai, Lower Sweep, stance.
You remain in the same position and do not move.

3. The Attacker steps forward with his right foot and strikes to Jodan, Upper, (Ganmen, the face) with his right fist.
You respond by pulling your right foot back and pulling your right fist back under your armpit. Use a Shuto, Knife Hand, to sweep the Attacker's wrist.

4. The Attacker remains in that position and does not move.
Grab the Attacker's wrist with your left hand. Pull him towards you and, as you do so, strike to Jodan, Upper, with your right fist.

	4. *Jodan Shuto Harai, Jodan Tsuki* **Upper Knife Hand Sweep, Upper Strike**
	5. The Attacker pulls his right foot back, returning to his original position. You step forward with your left foot, returning to your original position.
	6. The Attacker pulls his left foot back, moving his legs into Migi Zenkutsu Dachi, Right Front Stance. He pulls his left fist under his armpit and stands in Gedan Harai, Lower Sweep, stance. You remain in that position, not moving.
	7. The Attacker steps forward with his left foot and strike to Jodan, Upper, with his left fist. You respond by pulling your left foot back, and using a right Shuto, Knife Hand, to sweep the Attacker's wrist.
	8. The Attacker remains in that position, not moving. Grab the Attacker's wrist with your right hand. Pull him towards you and, as you do so, strike to Jodan, Upper, with your left fist.

（五）
上段揚受　中段突

前項の(8)の姿勢から突手は左足を引き、受手は左足を進めて、元の姿勢に戻る。

突手　右足を引き、左前屈立となり右拳を脇に下段拂の姿勢。

受手　そのまゝ動かず。

突手　右足を踏出し、右拳で上段を突く。

受手　右足を引き、右拳を脇下に、左拳の手首で敵の手を彈き揚げる。

突手　そのまゝ動かず。

受手　左拳を脇下に引くと同時に右拳で中段を突く。

突手　右足を引いて、元の
姿勢に戻る。
受手　右足を進めて元の姿
勢に戻る。

突手　左足を引き、右前屈
立となり、左拳を脇
に、下段拂の姿勢、
受手　そのまゝ動かず。

突手　左足を踏出し、左拳
で上段を突く。
受手　左足を引き、左拳を
脇下に、右拳の手首
で敵の手首を弾きあ
げる。

突手　そのまゝ動かず。
受手　右拳を脇下に引くと
同時に左拳で中段を
突く。

5. *Jodan Age-uke, Chudan Tsuki*
Upper Rising Block, Middle Strike

1. Continuing from step 8 of the previous technique, the Attacker pulls his left foot back while you, the Defender, step forward with your left foot. You both have returned to the starting position.

2. The Attacker pulls his right foot back, moving his legs into Hidari Zenkutsu Dachi, Left Front Stance. He pulls his right fist back under his armpit and stands in Gedan Harai, Lower Sweep Stance.
You remain in the same position and do not move.

3. The Attacker steps forward with his right foot and strikes to Jodan, Upper, with his right fist.
You respond by stepping back with your right foot and pulling your right fist below your armpit. With your left hand in a fist, swing your arm up and use your wrist to knock the opponent's hand up and away.

4. The Attacker remains in that position and does not move.
Pull your left fist back under your armpit and, at the same time, strike to Chudan, Middle, with your right fist.

5. *Jodan Age-uke, Chudan Tsuki*
Upper Rising Block, Middle Strike

5. The Attacker pulls his right foot back, returning to his original position.
You step forward with your right foot, returning to your original position.

6. The Attacker pulls his left foot back, moving his legs into Migi Zenkutsu Dachi, Right Front Stance. He pulls his left fist under his armpit and stands in Gedan Harai, Lower Sweep, stance.
You remain in that position, not moving.

7. The Attacker steps forward with his left foot and strikes to Jodan, Upper, with his left fist.
You respond by pulling your left foot back and moving your left fist below your armpit.

8. The Attacker remains in that position, not moving.
You pull your right fist underneath your armpit and, at the same time, strike to Chudan, Middle, with your left fist.

（六）
上段打込　中段突

前項の(8)の姿勢から突手は左足を引き、受手は左足を進めて、元の姿勢に戻る。

突手　右足を引き、左前屈立となり右拳を脇に下段拂の姿勢、

受手　そのまゝ動かず。

突手　右足を踏出し、右拳で上段を突く。

受手　左足を引き左拳を脇下に、右拳を振り上げぎま其手首で敵の腕を打ち落す。

突手　そのまゝ動かず。

受手　右拳を脇下に引くと同時に、左拳で中段を突く。

突手　右足を引いて元の姿勢に戻る。

受手　左足を進めて元の姿勢に戻る。

突手　左足を引き、右前屈立となり、左拳を脇に、下段拂の姿勢。

受手　そのまゝ動かず。

突手　左足を踏出し、左拳で上段を突く。

受手　右足を引き、右拳を脇下に、左拳を高く振り上げざま、其手首で敵の腕を打ち落す。

突手　そのまゝ動かず。

受手　左拳を脇下に引くと同時に右拳で中段を突く。

71

6. *Jodan Uchikomi, Chudan Tsuki*
Upper Deep Strike, Middle Strike

1. Continuing from step 8 of the previous technique, the Attacker pulls his left foot back while you, the Defender, step forward with your left foot. You both have returned to the starting position.

2. The Attacker pulls his right foot back, moving his legs into Hidari Zenkutsu Dachi, Left Front Stance. He pulls his right fist back under his armpit and stands in Gedan Harai, Lower Sweep Stance.
You remain in the same position and do not move.

3. The Attacker steps forward with his right foot and strikes Jodan, Upper, with his right fist.
You respond by pulling your left foot back and bringing your left fist under your armpit. Swing your right fist up like a pendulum, and strike the opponent's arm with your wrist. This is an Uchi Otoshi, Hit and Drop.

4. The Attacker remains in that position, not moving.
Pull your right fist back under your armpit and, at the same time, strike to Chudan, Middle, with your left fist.

6. *Jodan Uchikomi, Chudan Tsuki*
Upper Deep Strike, Middle Strike

	5. The Attacker pulls his right foot back, returning to his original position. You step forward with your right foot, returning to your original position.
	6. The Attacker pulls his left foot back, moving his legs into Migi Zenkutsu Dachi, Right Front Stance. He pulls his left fist back under his armpit and stands in Gedan Harai, Lower Sweep Stance. You remain in the same position and do not move.
	7. The Attacker steps forward with his left foot and strikes Jodan, Upper, with his left fist. You respond by pulling your right foot back and bringing your right fist under your armpit. Swing your left fist up like a pendulum, and strike the opponent's arm with your wrist. This is an Uchi Otoshi, Hit and Drop.
	8. The Attacker remains in that position, not moving. Pull your right fist back under your armpit and, at the same time, strike to Chudan, Middle, with your left fist.

會員番號一一〇六五

檢印

昭和十六年九月十八日印刷
昭和十六年九月二十日發行

增補空手道教範附圖
本圖ノミ　金三十錢

著者　富名腰義珍
東京市豊島區雑司ケ谷六ノ八一五

發行者　大倉克次
東京市京橋區京橋一丁目八番地

印刷者　高橋敏雄
東京市深川區扇橋下二丁目十五番地

發行所
東京市京橋區京橋一丁目八
振替東京四六八四　電話京橋六六

廣文堂書店

Printed September 18th Showa 16 (1941)
Published September 20th Showa 16

Author
Funakoshi Gichin

Translator's Note

The scrolls in the background are as follows:

		鹿島大明神 *Kashima Daimyoujin* The Kashima Great Lord of Light is the Saijin 祭神, or one of the deities enshrined at Kashima Shrine 鹿島神宮. This Shinto shrine is located in Ibaraki Prefecture. This deity is also known as Takemikazuchi-no-Ōkami 武甕槌大神 a patron saint of martial arts.
		香取大明神 *Katori Daimyoujin* The Katori Great Lord of Light is the Saijin of Katori Shrine. The deity is also known as Futsunushi 経津主神 the god of swords and lightning. Many martial arts dojos have a pair of scrolls showing the Kashima and Katori Daimyoujin.
		天照皇大神 *Amaterasu Sume O-Kami* Also known as Ameterasu, is the goddess of the sun in Japanese mythology. She first appears in the Kojiki written in 712 AD.